Snappers, Stingers and Stabbers of Australia

Ian Rohr

Published in Australia in 2006 by Young Reed
an imprint of New Holland Publishers (Australia) Pty Ltd
Sydney • Auckland • London • Cape Town

www.newholland.com.au

1/66 Gibbes Street Chatswood NSW 2067Australia
218 Lake Road Northcote Auckland New Zealand
86 Edgware Road London W2 2EA United Kingdom
80 McKenzie Street Cape Town 8001 South Africa

This edition published in 2010

National Library of Australia Cataloguing-in-Publication Data:
Rohr, Ian.
Snappers, stingers and stabbers of Australia.

Bibliography.
Includes index.
For primary school children.
ISBN 9781921580055.

1. Dangerous animals - Australia - Juvenile literature.
2. Poisonous animals - Australia - Juvenile literature. I.
Title.

591.650994

Publisher: Martin Ford
Project Editor: Yani Silvana
Educational Consultant: Joy Lawn
Designer: Tania Gomes
Production: Monique Layt
Printer: Toppan Leefung Printing Limited

Picture Credits
Abbreviations: t = top, b = bottom, l = left, r = right, c = centre, fp = full page

Allan Edgar: 6cl. **At A Glance**: 24b, 25t. **Barry Wilson**: 42tr. **beccasaunders.com.au**: 4–5fp, 11cr, 15br, 21cr, 29t, 36t, 39tr, 41t, 42bl, 43b. **Erik Schlogl**: 14b, 23tr. **Geoff Swan**: 7t, 9tr, 19t, 27b, 28tr, 28cr, 34tl, 34tr, 43t, back cover. **Guy Holt**: 39tl. **Jamie Seymour**: 11b. **Jill Simmons**: 33cr. **John Cooper**: 18c. **John Wombey**: 35b. **Ken Griffiths**: front cover bl, 1l, 6b, 13c, 26t, 26cl, 27t, 27c, 28l, 28b, 29c, 29b. **Lisa-Ann Gershwin**: 5tr. **Lochman Transparencies**: Clay Bryce 10t, 41b; Geoff Taylor 13br; Gunther Schmida 23tc; Dennis Sarson 26b; Hans&Judy Beste 40–41fp; Peter Marsack 40t; Dave Watts 42tl. **marinethemes.com**: Clay Bryce 5tl; Kelvin Aitken front cover t, 4bl, 10–11fp, 11tr, 15t, 20–21fp, 21bl, 21br; Mark Conlin 21tl; David Fleetham 23br; Steve Drogin 42fp. **markspencer.com.au**: 39b. **Museum Victoria/Alan Henderson**: 35t. **Neil Vincent**: 5b, 8fp, 11tl, 12–13fp, 14t, 22–23fp, 22b, 23tl, 23bl, 23bcr, 38–39fp, 39cr, 40b, 47. **New Holland Image Library**: 2–3, 6tl, 6tr, 7br, 9tl, 11tc, 22bl, 24–25fp, 24tl, 25cr, 25br, 26fp, 30–31, 44. **Paul Zborowski**: front cover br, 1r, 7cl, 8b, 9bl, 9br, 9cr, 16, 17tr, 17cl, 17cr, 18b, 19b, 32, 33 (except cr), 34fp, 34br, 35br, 36fp, 37. **Rob Valentic**: 41c. **Sophie Edgar**: 18t. **Steve Wilson**: 17b.

The names of the main animals shown in this book are in **bold**. Other bold words are explained in the glossary.

Contents

Meet the Wild Bunch

Some of Australia's wildest inhabitants are massive, others are minuscule. Some make you ill, others can kill. But despite their weaponry these animals aren't out to 'get' you. Most will avoid humans. Most will only sting or bite in self-defence. Even what may seem like a deliberate attack can turn out to be a case of mistaken identity. When it comes to Australia's more dangerous animals you should certainly be alert, but there's no need to be alarmed. Lurking around these pages are some of our wilder animals. Some you'll recognise, but others may come as a bit of a surprise.

Vivid and Venomous

They might look like plants but **corals** are made up of colonies animals—carnivorous animals called coral polyps. The hard stuff we call coral is actually the home that the polyps build for themselves. The polyps are armed with stinging cells to kill their prey. Contact with some of their tentacles can prove painful for divers and swimmers.

Shells that Strike

Don't let the striking markings fool you. The thing that lives inside this **cone shell** is able to swiftly shoot out a **venom**-squirting dart. And no matter how you pick it up or hold it, this harpoon can twist and turn to stab you. And it could kill you.

Shiny Stingers

Shimmery tentacles streaming metres behind them as they swim through the sea, these fragile-looking creatures pack a powerful punch. One of the deadliest creatures found in Australian marine environments, **Box Jellyfish** are dangerous enough to make our northern beaches off-limits to swimmers for half of the year.

White-tipped Reef Sharks *are not usually dangerous to humans, although occasionally they have bitten divers or spearfishers when excited by bait in the water.*

Sea Shadows

There are over 160 **species** of shark in our waters, but only a few pose any real threat to people. Even so, many Australians feel uneasy while treading water in salt water. But humans kill millions of sharks every year, making people much more dangerous to sharks than sharks are to us.

Blue for Danger

Bold, bright colours in nature often mean 'danger, back off' and this **Blue-ringed Octopus's** dazzling rings are no exception. Although it can only give a small bite, its powerful **venom** can kill an adult human.

Funnel-web Fear

This is one wild Australian that it's best to avoid. **Funnel-web spiders** are large and can be aggressive. They are also quite capable of injecting a lethal dose of **venom**. But they won't attack unprovoked with the intention of biting you, despite many people's fear of this occurring.

The Venom Factor

Is a snake poisonous? No, it isn't. Can a snake poison you? Yes, a venomous one can, if it bites you. A poisonous animal is only dangerous if you eat it. A venomous animal produces **venom** to kill its prey. Venom is often strong enough to do us serious harm because it's designed to kill prey quickly—otherwise the prey might get away or, worse, fight back and hurt the hunter. It's just bad luck for us that venom made to kill mostly mice and other small creatures can have the same deadly effect on humans. So, you can eat a snake safely—just make sure you cook it first.

Dingo Danger?

You might think a wild **Dingo** would be more dangerous than one that is used to humans. But no—tame or semi-wild dingoes can be riskier to be around. Wild animals that have a lot of contact with people lose their fear of us. They can also start expecting that every person they come across is going to throw them some picnic scraps. If this doesn't happen, the animal can get aggressive.

Snakes and Us

Few Australians encounter a snake in the wild without taking a step backwards. With their sleek shape and flicking tongues, snakes inspire fear in many people. But most snakes are shy and will get out of your way just as long as they know you're coming through.

Like all brown snakes, this ***Western Brown Snake*** *is dangerous. Stay away!*

This Creature Can Kill

When we think of deadly and dangerous creatures, bees are probably not what first springs to mind. Unless, of course, you are allergic to bee stings. The introduced common **European Honeybee** kills more people in Australia each year than spiders and snakes put together.

Tiny and Troublesome

The tiny **tick** can burrow deep down into your skin without you even noticing. Losing the few drops of blood that the tick is sucking out won't harm you, but the **toxins** it injects into your bloodstream might. They can lead to illness and, in severe cases, paralysis.

A Powerful Predator

Billabongs, rivers and swamps around Australia's tropical north coast are home to **Saltwater Crocodiles** up to 7 metres long. You'll even find them swimming in the sea. Crocodile attacks are rare, but when one occurs it taps into our ancient fears of being hunted and devoured by a big hungry predator.

Proceed with Caution

Having an unwanted encounter with wild Australia often comes down to being in the wrong place at the wrong time. If you make an animal feel threatened, either accidentally or deliberately, perhaps by trying to pick it up or hit it, it will react as best it can. Many will simply run, slither or fly off. Others might not, especially if surprised or cornered. But what might seem like an attack to you is often self-defence from the animal's point of view. Because of this it is worth knowing where you're likely to find some of our more dangerous animals, if only to reduce the risk of any unplanned get-togethers.

Beware the Rock Pool

Danger sometimes lurks in the prettiest places and takes the most attractive forms. Blue-ringed Octopuses are just one reason why you should look but not touch when it comes to rock pools. These creatures usually only bite when disturbed, stood on or picked up. And they like to hide in shells and old bottles. Many rock-pool dwellers are fragile and easily injured by groping human hands.

Life Under Logs

A rotting log is an ideal habitat for many different animals. So never put your hands under fallen timber without first checking that there is nothing lurking beneath. The same goes for large rocks, and as for sticking your bare hands into holes and crevices, don't even think about it. Also, step up onto large logs rather than straight over them— a snake could be on the other side.

Something Likes Living Here

Many spider **species** relish damp humid places. That is why you should always wear thick gloves and take care when digging around foundations, drains or in shady corners of the yard. The dangerous funnel-web spider is **nocturnal** and usually encountered on warm summer nights. But if you disturb their burrow under a rock or log during the day they are likely to emerge with fangs bared and **venom** ready to squirt.

Safety and Sharks

To avoid shark attacks don't :

- swim at dusk or night-time, or among schools of fish, or in murky water or water that swiftly drops from shallow to deep
- swim if you're bleeding
- splash around a lot
- take your dog swimming with you.

What's in the Woodpile?

Warm, dry, snug—stacks of wood or iron make ideal habitats for some snake **species**. When you're getting wood or lifting sheets of iron, wear gloves and move objects towards rather than away from you. That way if something is underneath, it can escape on the other side. Make a noise so creatures know you're around.

Safe Strolling

No matter how hot it gets, you should never walk through the bush or thick grassy areas barefoot or in thongs. Stout boots, thick socks and long pants will help protect the parts of you that are most likely to come close to a snake, or a spider, or a centipede, or any other nippers.

*This **paper wasp** is collecting water from a bird bath to help make the paper for its nest.*

Drink of Death?

It's not just the sugar in the soft drink that's bad for you. Wasps and bees, attracted by the sweetness, will sometimes crawl into a can unnoticed. A sting inside your throat, with its associated swelling, can be dangerous so keep food and drink containers covered when you're outdoors.

Toxic Tattoo

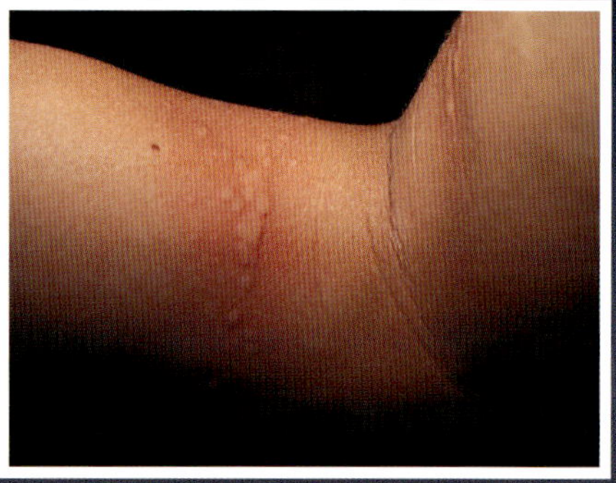

The bad news is that **Box Jellyfish** stings are at worst deadly and at least extremely painful. The good news is that there is an antivenom. When the stinging cells on the tentacles are stimulated by a fish, a crustacean, or human skin, the **venom** is injected via a coiled thread or hook inside the **nematocyst**. You can be wrapped in dozens of tentacles, coated with thousands of nematocysts, all of them pumping away. And you can be left with permanent scarring.

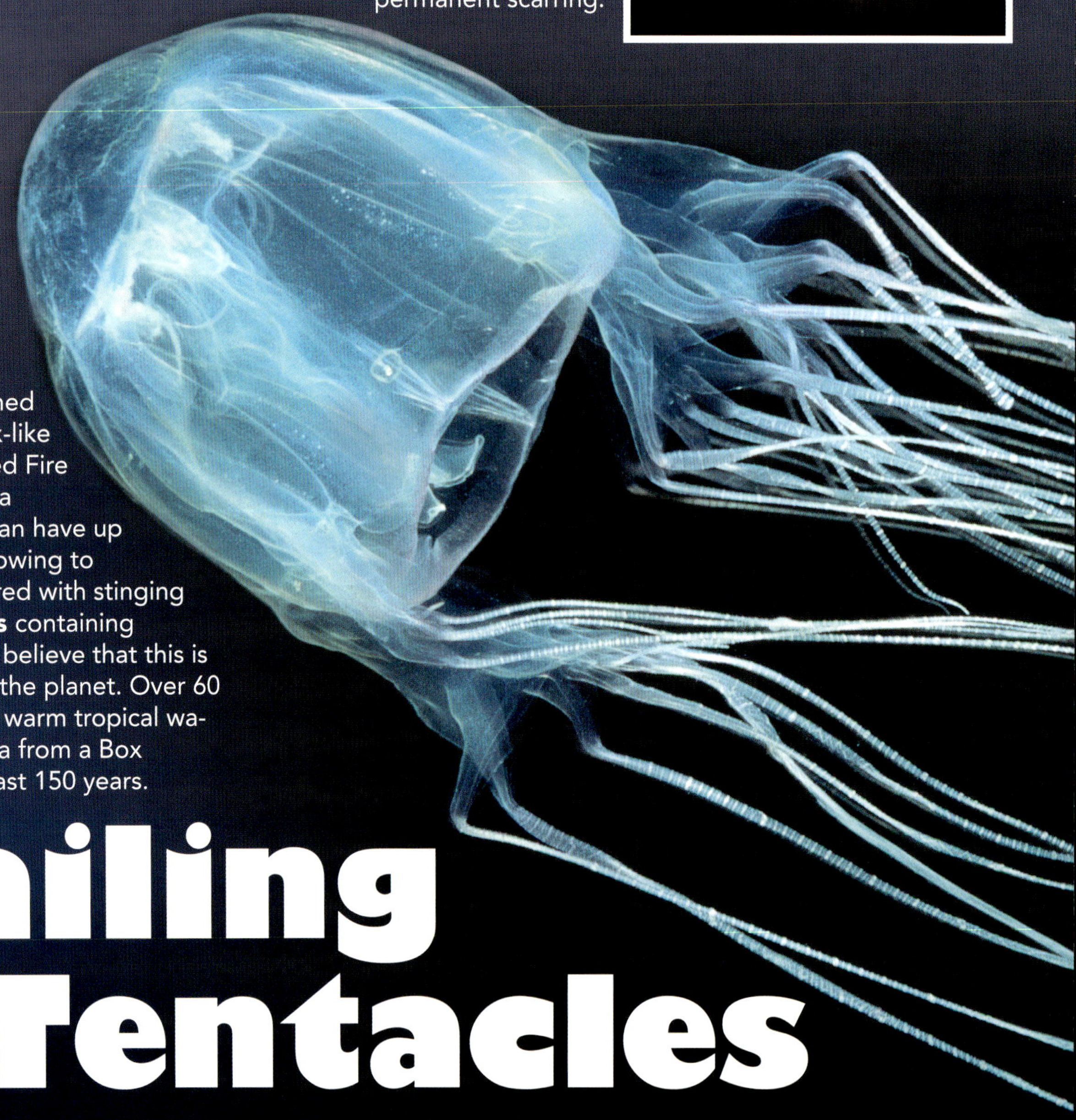

Box of Bother

The **Box Jellyfish** is named for its four-cornered box-like shape. They're also called Fire Medusas and Deadly Sea Wasps. A Box Jellyfish can have up to 50 tentacles, each growing to 3 metres long and covered with stinging cells called **nematocysts** containing **venom**. Some scientists believe that this is the deadliest animal on the planet. Over 60 people have died in the warm tropical waters of northern Australia from a Box Jellyfish sting over the last 150 years.

Trailing Tentacles

Every summer some unlucky beachgoers have a lovely day turn memorable for the wrong reasons. One minute they are happily splashing and swimming, the next they're running from the water screaming and shouting. Why? Well, they may have tangled with the tentacles of one of Australia's dangerous jellyfish species. Jellyfish are cnidarians (pronounced nid-AIR-ee-ans) and are related to coral and sea anemones. All cnidarians have some form of stinger that they use to catch and kill their prey, but not all cnidarians are harmful to humans.

Not One but Many

A **Bluebottle**, also called a Portuguese Man-of-war, looks like a single brightly coloured **iridescent** creature, but there's more to them than that. Each one is made up of separate **organisms** that join together to form a **colony**, consisting of a float and stinging and feeding tentacles. Like all **cnidarians**, Bluebottles use their **venom** to kill and help digest their prey.

A ***Bluebottle*** *can still sting you even when it's been washed ashore and is dead. So look, but don't touch.*

Stay Cool in the Pool

In some parts of Australia's tropical north netted beaches provide some protection from larger jellyfish. But bits of broken tentacles can get through the gaps and sting you. A small piece of tentacle can have enough **nematocysts** and **venom** to give a painful and potentially dangerous sting. And the tiny Irukandjis are not put off by the mesh—they often slip straight through. So stay cool and swim in a pool.

Underwater Fire

Fire corals are not true corals but they can truly sting. Related to true corals and jellyfish, they use their nematocysts to catch small prey swimming by. If a diver or swimmer brushes up against the fire coral it can lead to a painful, itchy sting.

Almost Invisible

Irukandjis are about as tiny as a toenail but they deliver a painful and occasionally deadly sting. Found mainly in the tropics, they can be almost impossible to see when you look down into that crystal clear water. So if they might be around, stay dry.

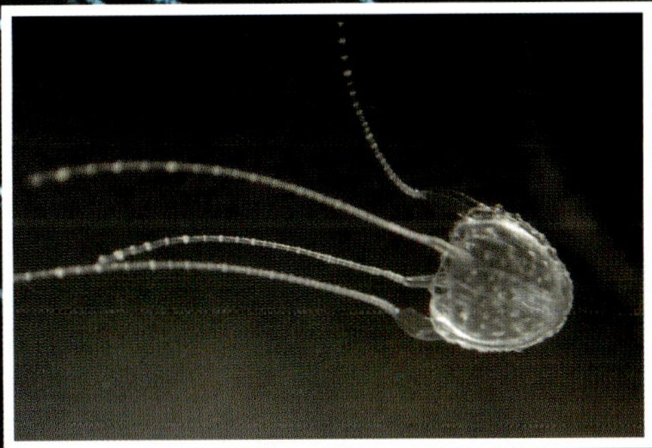

Burning Butterfly

The bright colours and feathery fins of a **Butterfly Cod** have tempted many a diver or snorkeller to come closer. But another name for this striking creature is the Firefish, which should give you an idea of the burning sensation a sting from one of its 13 spines will cause.

Fiery Fish

Did you know that putting your foot on a fish could be fatal? When we think of dangerous fish we usually think of the big ones, or frenzied snapping schools, but smaller fish can be dangerous too. It's best to look before you leap and keep your hands and feet to yourself when close to anything from the scorpion fish **family**. If you don't, you could end up with a painful puncture, or worse, from their **venom**-filled spikes.

Serious Spikes

Defence is vital in the animal world. Most things are a potential meal for something else. To frighten any nudging nosy fish away the **Stonefish** raises its 13 hollow spikes, and these can easily pierce even through sand-shoes into your soft feet. Because Stonefish are often semi-hidden under the sand in the shallows, watch where you're walking when wading through water. You don't want to tread on a Stonefish!

Stay Away from the Stone

The spikes lying flat on a **Stonefish**'s back have nothing to do with it getting food. Its big mouth takes care of that. Looking like a resting rock, this 30-centimere **camouflaged** creature lies in wait in Australia's tropical seas. When a fish swims too close or a prawn passes by, it opens wide, sucks in and gulps down.

This **Porcupine Fish** *is covered in spines and doesn't look very good to eat.*

From Hook to Cook to Crook!

A venomous fish injects you with a poison. A poisonous fish make you sick if you eat it. Some of the poisoners you might find on your fishing line include Toadfish, Pufferfish and **Porcupine Fish**. To help make sure you're not tempted to taste, many poisonous fish also puff themselves up and don't look like something you'd want on your dinner plate.

Watch Out for the Bullrout

If you think you're safe walking in freshwater rivers and creeks, think again. The **Bullrout** is similar to the Stonefish but lives in fresh water. It can also inflict a painful wound from its defensive spikes. So keep your thick-soled shoes on. As with many stings from the scorpion-fish **family**, placing the injured limb in very hot water can do a lot to relieve the pain and reduce the **venom**'s effects.

Shock Tactics

Electric rays like the **Torpedo Ray** can deliver a jolt of electricity to scare off predators and help capture their prey. The electric fields they produce also help them to 'see' their surroundings. Torpedo Rays can discharge up to 220 volts of electricity from their internal electric organs. A big shock could knock you down, which wouldn't be too good if you're in the water. These rays are often caught on fishing lines and in nets and most shocks to humans occur when they are being removed. Just like **venom**, after the electricity is discharged the animal must slowly replenish its reservoir.

Fiery Fortescues

Fortescues have more spikes than Stonefish, but these smaller stabbers are not as dangerous. Even so, if you tread on one or pick it up, you'll soon wish you hadn't. Rarely bigger than 15 centimetres, these small, mottled fish are often caught by people after prawns and other fish, so if you like fishing, wear thick gloves.

Buzzers, Biters and Bombers

It's not always the big creatures that you need to be aware of. Many a picnic has been plagued by biting bugs and swarming sand-flies. While these **insects** are usually more annoying than dangerous, some of Australia's stingers have very painful ways of making intruders retreat. Some crawl along the ground, or up your leg, others fight on the wing. Most only become aggressive if they or their nests are disturbed, but a mass attack is frightening, painful and potentially dangerous.

Back Off from Bull Ants

Don't park yourself near a **Bull Ant**'s nest. Bull Ants are big, up to 3 centimetres long, and will swarm out to attack anything troubling the nest or interfering with any outside worker ants. Hundreds of ants may rush to the defence of a threatened individual. The **mandibles** look frightening, and they do hurt when they latch on, but it's the stinger and **venom** at the other end of the ant that causes the more memorable pain. Of the 4000 or so ant **species** in Australia, Bulldog Ants, Jumper Ants and the introduced Red Fire Ants are also common, and painful, biters and stingers.

Lots of Wasps

Yes, there are lots of wasps out there: hundreds of different **species**, millions of individuals. Many of these species, both native and introduced, will sting repeatedly to defend their nests. Some species, such as the introduced European Wasp, often descend in a swarm to protect their large **communal** home. Though a single sting is painful, it is the combined effect of multiple jabs that is usually responsible for a bad allergic reaction.

Paper wasps *will sting nastily when protecting their papery nests.*

Introduced Wasp

The **European Wasp** has only been here since the late 1950s but it has managed to make itself at home over much of southern Australia. Easily identified by the bold black and yellow markings, European Wasps usually build their nests in trees, hollow logs or underground, as well as in ceilings, walls and eaves. Since thousands of wasps can inhabit a single large nest, and humans and wasps don't make good neighbours, the best thing to do is get your parents to call in professional exterminators.

Edible Ants

Here's an ant you can bite back if it bites you. The **abdomen** has a pleasant lemony taste. Aborigines would boil up a whole nest of these ants to produce a warm soothing drink high in vitamin C that they used to treat colds and sore throats. Common in the tropics, brightly coloured **Green Tree Ants** construct their nests in trees by gluing leaves together. With all the effort they put into building the nest, it's not surprising that they'll rush out in a mass to attack anything threatening it or the tree. The multiple bites can be painful but luckily no **venom** is injected.

Unwelcome Introduced Ant

If you live around Brisbane, watch out for Fire Ants! They'll give you a fiery sting that causes a nasty blister. They build their often-mounded nests up to 40 centimetres high in open areas such as your backyard. The ants are aggressive and have a stinger on the tail. Some people think they're the worst thing to happen to Australia since the Cane Toad. They bite people, kill native animals, and damage crops and even electrical wiring. Queensland authorities are trying to get rid of them, but it's not easy.

Bird Bombers

Magpie Missiles

A bike ride to the shops or a stroll to school can take a startling turn in spring, the Magpie nesting season. These black and white bombers will dive repeatedly to try and drive what they see as a dangerous intruder away from the nest area. The sudden clacking of a beak, the beating of wings and a rush of air is often the last minute 'look out' warning as the Magpie strikes. Though most of these sneak attacks will only give you a fright, Magpies occasionally make contact and draw blood. Other Australian birds that will swoop to protect their nests or young are the Noisy Miner, the Grey Butcherbird and the Red Wattlebird.

Protective Plovers

Plovers are plucky when it comes to defending their young. Though their nests are on the ground they'll swiftly take to the air to swoop down on anyone or anything they think is walking too close to the eggs or nestlings. If the squawking and flapping wings aren't enough to drive you away, they also have sharp wing spurs for added persuasion. Like most nesting birds, this **Masked Lapwing** (one **species** of plover) will let you get to within 30–50 metres of its nest before it swoops into action.

Honey and Venom

A sting from a **European Honeybee** can occasionally be fatal: about 25 people die each year in Australia from either multiple stings, or a single sting to which they've had an allergic reaction. But the sting is always fatal to the bee. The bee's sting has a barb on the end that embeds itself into flesh. When the bee flies off, the sting is ripped from its body, **disembowelling** it and leaving you with a little sac of **venom** attached. When removing the sting take special care to not squeeze the sac or you'll inject more venom into your body. Most native bees are less aggressive and have smaller stings, but the absence of barbs allows them to sting and survive to sting again, and again.

Night-time Hunters

Australia's biggest **centipede** grows to 14 centimetres long. It hunts spiders, frogs, **insects** and even small snakes, and with 30–40 pairs of legs it can produce some pace when in pursuit of its prey. Centipedes are **nocturnal** and in their nightly hunt for food can follow scent trails into shoes, clothes and sleeping bags. Their bites are painful enough to make it worth the effort to shake out any shoes or clothing left on the floor overnight. Unlike their shyer relatives, the stinging scorpions, centipedes are as likely to advance and bite as retreat when something gets in their way.

Armed Assassin

You don't want to be an **Assassin Bug's** prey. Once it has impaled the prey to hold it steady, it pumps in a salivary secretion that immobilises it and starts to dissolve its internal tissues. The Assassin Bug then sucks up this 'soup', leaving a dry hollow shell. Bites to people can be painful, with intense burning followed by an itchy lump, but it rarely gets any worse than this, unlike it does for the Assassin Bug's prey.

Slash and Slice

There's only one way to guarantee you'll never be attacked by a shark: never go near the water. But you'll be missing out on a lot of fun for a tiny risk. The fear of attack is understandable, but it's rare that anyone will see that dark triangle slicing through the water. Considering the number of people who spend time in and on the world's oceans, rivers and harbours, it's surprising there aren't more attacks. There certainly would be more if sharks seriously hunted us like they hunt their prey. But the 100 or so unprovoked attacks a year, resulting in about 10–15 deaths, would suggest that's not the case. Maybe we're more interested in sharks than they are in us.

The Well-known White

There are over 350 **species** of sharks swimming around worldwide. Of them all, the **Great White** is probably the best known. It has starred in movies, been tagged by researchers, filmed for documentaries and killed by human hunters. On rare occasions it hunts us. To be suddenly attacked by a Great White would be a terrible, terrifying experience. But after that first thump and bite the Great White often swims away from a human. Unfortunately, their size, strength and huge sharp teeth mean that what might just be a taste test to them can be fatal to us.

How Great Whites Find their Prey

1. Smell: Great Whites can detect 1 part blood in 1 000 000 000 parts of water—like a drop of blood in an Olympic-sized swimming pool. The shark may choose to follow the blood to its source.

2. Hearing: Great Whites can hear the low-frequency sounds of a struggling, wounded creature from about a kilometre away.

3. Distant touch: Lines along the shark's side, known as lateral lines, contain sensory cells that allow the shark to pick up splashing and swimming sounds from about 200 metres away. You probably wouldn't even know it was nearby, but the shark knows you're there.

4. Sight: As the shark circles closer to an object it can see the thing that attracted it. Once convinced that it's prey, the shark charges in.

5. Electric vision: As the shark nears, its eyes roll back to protect them from injury during the attack, and tiny electro-sensitive organs in the snout take over for the final moments. Picking up the electrical field given off by the prey, these organs perform the last action in guiding the Great White to its food.

Shark Alleyways

Most sharks stick to the sea but the **Bull Shark** can inhabit many **aquatic** environments. From murky shallows to way upstream in freshwater rivers, the Bull Shark can appear in unexpected places. Aggressive 3-metre Bull Sharks sometimes appear in the built canals of the Gold Coast, chasing schools of fish that think they have found themselves a nice, safe habitat. Two fatal attacks in recent years have raised awareness that the Bull Shark is one to be wary of.

Well-hidden Wobbegongs

Well-**camouflaged Wobbegongs** often wait on the sea floor for a fish to swim by. Their mottled brown, yellow and grey skin blends into the background. When something edible comes within reach the Wobbegong uses the worm-like threads around its mouth to suck in the prey to where the shark's small, sharp teeth are waiting. Attacks on humans are rare but the 3-metre Wobbegong's habit of grabbing hold and not letting go can definitely add to the trauma.

Circle or Strike?

The **Tiger Shark** can be a bit of a garbage guts. Tiger Shark stomach contents have contained everything from sheep heads to empty bottles to smaller, slower Tiger Sharks. From time to time, they contain human remains. Tiger Sharks grow to 5 metres but can often seem timid, sometimes circling prey for hours, long after it is dead, before closing in. At other times, they'll launch a sudden surprise attack. Though they prefer tropical waters Tiger Sharks can also be found down the east and west coasts of Australia.

Watch Out for Whalers

Whalers are named from the days when they followed whaling boats to feed on the harpooned whales. There is no longer any whaling in Australian waters, but there are still whaler sharks. Both the Dusky and **Bronze Whalers** (below) have been known to attack humans and, like their relative the Bull Shark, they often frequent shallow water.

A Munch from a Moray

A bite from a big eel usually leaves a torn, jagged, bleeding wound, sometimes minus a chunk of flesh. What makes eel bites so unpleasant is the method they use to tear meat off larger prey. By tying their own tails into a knot, and using this as a support, they twist around and rip away, taking a big piece of flesh with them. Because blood loss is accelerated underwater, stopping the bleeding is often the first priority.

Wrigglers and Wrappers

Giant octopuses grabbing screaming sailors with their tentacles and enormous eels emerging from gloomy caves seeking divers for dinner—these are fiction, not fact. There are few real cases of unprovoked octopus or eel attacks on humans. Still, both creatures are armed predators and natural hunters and swimmers, so respect them and give them space when you are in the water.

Nimble Nippers

Crayfish Clutch

You wouldn't call a **Yabby** dangerous but you might call it painful. These small 7–20-centimetre freshwater crayfish use their pincers to catch their prey. If you happen to get hold of a Yabby you might find that, in self-defence, the Yabby has also gotten a hold of you.

Clinging Claws

Mud Crabs can grow to 30 centimetres across. If they grab your finger or toe with their claw, it can take a hammer to remove it. And if the claw snaps off, the crab simply scuttles away, leaving it behind, still firmly attached to you.

That's A Moray

A **Moray Eel**, hovering half-in and half-out of its hole, doesn't look too approachable. But these usually shy, mostly nocturnal eels can grow quite 'tame' when they become accustomed to people. They can even get used to being fed by hand. But if you swim up with no food for the expectant eel it might take a swipe at thc hand that didn't feed it.

Beware other eels too (below)—they can also bite!

Reef-dwelling ***Conger Eels*** *grow up to 3 metres long and are easily irritated. You wouldn't want to tangle with a conger.*

You're more likely to tread on a ***Freshwater Eel*** *in a river than be bitten by one, though they can give a painful nip.*

An Arsenal for Attacks

Octopuses and their relatives the squid use their tentacles and suckers to grab and hold their prey. They use their strong, sharp beaks to kill it and pull it apart. Many **species** can also inject **venom**, helping them to make a swifter, safer kill.

Scary though it looks, This ***Sydney Common Octopus*** *is unlikely to be dangerous to humans—but it can paral-yse its prey with venom.*

The venom-filled bite of this ***Blue-ringed Octopus*** *is deadly. It has caught and killed a Decorator Crab. Can you tell what's crab and what's octopus? Beware 'empty' shells and bottles as they make good homes for Blue-ringeds.*

This ***Day Octopus*** *is escaping under cover of a cloud of its squirted 'ink'. Many octopuses and squids can perform this trick—alarming, but not harmful.*

Snap and Twirl

With a powerful lunge the **Estuarine** (or Saltwater) Crocodile bursts from the **billabong**, grabbing a drinking wallaby by the throat. Almost as quickly as it appeared, the croc is back in the water. In what's known as a 'death roll' it spins the wallaby around and around under the water to drown it swiftly. In less than a minute the wallaby's struggles are over. A hungry Estuarine Crocodile will ambush or chase down a menu of marine creatures as well as any land animal, us included, that is unwary or unfortunate enough to wander down to the water's edge when a croc is waiting.

Small, Slim Strikers

The **Freshwater Crocodile** gets a lot less attention than its much larger and more dangerous relative, the **Estuarine** Crocodile. 'Freshies', as they're known up north, have narrower jaws well designed for catching fish, turtles and other **aquatic** prey. They'll usually only attack when provoked, and they do much less damage.

Safe Swimming

If you spend time in Australia's tropical north you'll get used to seeing these signs. But don't assume that no sign means no crocs. Saltwater Crocodiles can be found in most bodies of water across northern Australia and not all will be signposted. Ask the locals where it's safe to swim and you should stay fine without the sign. And don't think that fresh water is alright either. The name Saltwater Crocodile is misleading: they can be found in salty, **brackish** and fresh water.

Mum's the Word

Female crocodiles might be capable killers but they are also devoted mothers. Although many of the 50 or so eggs the female lays will never hatch, the ones that do are carried from the nest to the water by their mother. They will stay around her for the next few months. Many will be taken by predators, but Mum's presence will help ensure that some survive.

*This female **Saltie** is guarding her nest constructed of leaves and grasses (background).*

From Egg to Adult

It's either a long hard struggle for a crocodile to get from the egg to fully grown or a life cut swiftly short. Whole clutches of eggs may be destroyed by floods or overheating and feral pigs and goannas like to eat them. Only about 20 of every 100 will hatch, and birds, fish and bigger crocodiles will take a heavy toll of those that make it to the water. Less than 1 per cent of the hatchlings that struggle from the shell will make it to maturity.

Hidden Hunter

How can a creature so suited to life in the water be such a successful predator of land-based creatures? A combination of stealth, surprise, speed and strength are what enable **Saltwater Crocodiles** to grab and overpower land animals, large and small. A crocodile will glide just under the water's surface right up to the bank without causing a ripple. With a sudden, surprising leap from the water the prey is in its clutches. The croc's strength enables it to drag a creature as big as a buffalo back under and drown it.

*This **Saltie** is leaping out of the water to grab a piece of meat dangled off a tourist boat in the Northern Territory.*

Prehistoric Predators

Most animals attack humans in defence of themselves, their young or their territory. But **Saltwater Crocodiles** will also attack because they see us as prey. Growing from 5 to 7 metres long, these biggest of the reptiles are formidable predators. Crocodile attacks are rare, about two a year, with one every couple of years proving fatal.

Show of Seriousness

A snake's threat display, with the body reared up into an s-shape, mouth wide open and making repeated strikes, usually puts off all but the most persistent pursuers. Many snakes choose this method of driving off a threat in order to save **venom** for when they really need it. The likelihood that many snakes will use a threat display or **dry bite** instead of a genuine attack helps reduce the risk to humans.

Red and Black Attack

The glistening **Red-bellied Black Snake** is striking in appearance, but not so likely to strike out at a human. Red-bellieds are responsible for many bites, but mainly because they are found over much of eastern Australia where the majority of people also live. Despite the number of Red-bellied bites, none has ever proven fatal. Unlike some of our more dangerous snakes, the Red-bellied's **venom** doesn't cause paralysis or internal bleeding. Having said that, a bite would still make you feel very unwell, and probably wishing you had taken a few simple snake bite-avoidance measures, like wearing thick socks and shoes in the bush.

This **brown snake** *is in attack mode.*

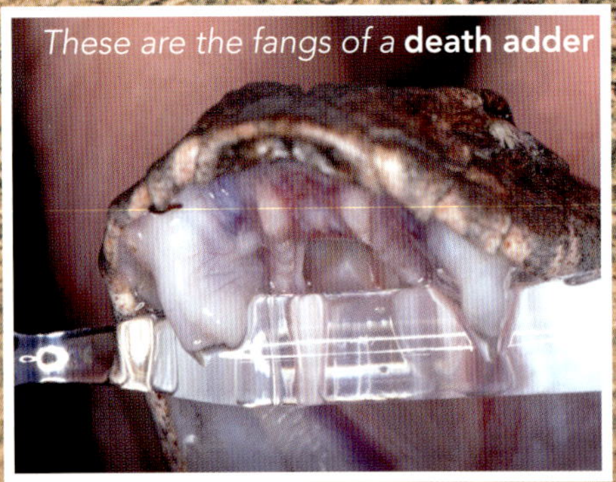

These are the fangs of a **death adder**

Fearsome Fangs

Snakes use their fangs to pump **venom** into another creature. Like hypodermic needles, they direct the venom to where it will act swiftly, circling through the prey's body in its bloodstream. But not all bites will result in death or even illness. The snake can choose whether or not to inject venom, and how much to release. Venom is precious, so bites designed to repel rather than kill are often dry, with no venom injected.

Lifesaving Liquid—What is Antivenom?

Antivenoms are substances developed by humans to reverse or reduce the effects of **venom** from snakes and other dangerous creatures. Antivenom is usually produced by giving animals such as sheep or horses small doses of a particular venom until they develop **antibodies** to fight off that poison's effects. Blood is then extracted from the animal and the antibodies it has produced are used to make the antivenom.

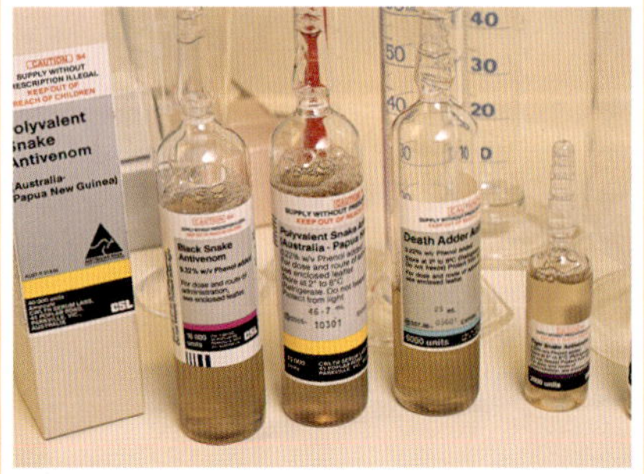

Swift-striking Slitherers

When you think of Australia's wildest creatures what first creeps into your mind? Snakes are what slither into many people's imagination, and with 25 Australian **species** classed as 'potentially deadly' it might seem like there's a lot to worry about. But the 'potentially' is important. Most snakes prefer to save their **venom** up for genuine prey, rather than waste it repelling a threat. All the snakes on these pages produce sufficient quantities of venom to kill people but most will choose to slip off into the undergrowth if they can.

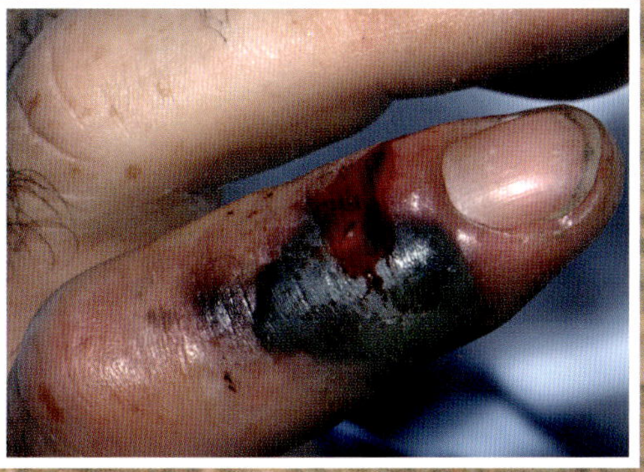

This is the result of a bite from a ***black snake****.*

Bad Bites

Pain, paralysis, vomiting and cramps: the effects of **venom** vary. Some venom is specialised to attack the nervous system, producing paralysis. Other types attack the muscle cells, causing heart or kidney failure, while some affect the blood's ability to clot, causing major internal bleeding. But all are designed to quickly and cleanly kill prey.

Deathly Adder

With a name like '**death adder**', you'd be foolish to fool with these snakes. They're short and squat and they pack a mean punch. They hide among leaf litter, soil or sand and wait for prey to pass by. Humans usually get bitten when they stray too close, often at night. Despite the death adder's grim name, antivenom has drastically reduced the human toll resulting from this squat snake's swift strike.

Tangles with Tigers

Tiger Snakes don't mind getting wet. Often found around creeks and swamps in cooler parts of the country, Tiger Snakes are named for the distinctive coloured bands that many of them have. Their colours range from black through brown, olive, yellow and grey. All are potentially dangerous. Until the development of antivenom in the 1930s half the victims of Tiger Snake bite died, usually from paralysis, internal bleeding, muscle damage, or a killer combination of all of these conditions.

Give Snakes a Break

Though many people are frightened of them there's a lot to be said for snakes. Without them, we would have many more rats and other rodents. Snakes help keep pest populations at a reasonable level. And **venom** isn't just a bad thing. Doctors are studying its effects to see if it can be used in helping treat or reverse human diseases, with encouraging results for afflictions such as epilepsy and multiple sclerosis.

When snakes like this ***Tiger Snake*** *come too close to people's homes, expert reptile handlers remove them and return them to their natural environment, a safer option both for them and for us.*

Mulgas Make More Venom

The **Mulga Snake** produces the largest amount of **venom** of any Australian snake—good news for the snake, bad news for its prey. Growing up to 3 metres long, the Mulga's venom-producing ability makes it potentially dangerous. Another common name for the Mulga is the King Brown, but this is misleading. Though it accurately reflects the snake's size and typical colour, Mulga Snakes are members of the black snake **genus**.

Sought-after Snake

Even people who go looking for this ghostly looking nighttime hunter rarely spot one. Found along parts of the east coast, the elusive **Pale-headed Snake** avoids contact with humans, including researchers who want to learn more about it. Though it is not known to have caused any human deaths, its **venom** is toxic and presumed dangerous. In this case and many others, where we have insufficient **species** to study, we can only suspect that the venom is dangerous because we know it is in the case of their closest relatives.

Where Browns are Found

The '**brown snake**' is a plain and simple name for a snake that comes in a range of colours and markings. Brown snakes can be anything from almost black to the palest of browns, along with grey and orange. There are about six dangerous **species** in Australia. Some, such as Western Australia's Dugite or South Australia's Spotted Brown, are restricted to small, localised areas. Others are much more widespread: between the pair of them the **Eastern** (pictured) and Western browns have most of the country covered, with the exception of Tasmania.

Snakes in the Sea

Not only does it sometimes seem like we live on a continent crawling with venomous snakes, but they can also be found in the sea. But although their **venom** is potent, sea snakes have small fangs, and **dry bites** are common. A freely swimming sea snake rarely bites: it's those caught on fishing lines or in nets that are most likely to strike.

Olive Sea Snake

Big Snake, Big Bite

Taipans are big snakes (3 metres long) with big fangs and lots of potent **venom** to inject. A taipan will rarely stand its ground, but when it does, this snake is well equipped to do so. Repeated strikes can result in a massive dose of venom entering the bloodstream and, until an antivenom came on the scene, nearly all victims of a taipan bite died.

The Victimless Killer

How can the world's deadliest snake have not caused any human deaths? Based on the **toxicity** of its **venom**, the **Inland Taipan** is the world's most lethal land snake but there are no recorded fatalities from the **species**. This is due to the combination of a shy nature, a reluctance to strike and the fact that its habitat is in a remote part of inland Australia.

Hogs Gone Wild

Wild boars shouldn't be members of Australia's wild bunch, but they are. Mostly descended from escaped domestic pigs, their habit of digging up vast areas of ground in their search for edible roots is destructive to many native plants and animals. Large pigs, both male and female, can have impressive tusks so if one threatens, scramble up the nearest tree. Quickly.

Coat-of-arms Kicker

We tend to think of kangaroos as cuddly, harmless creatures. But a cornered kangaroo will stand up to an attacker as a last ditch measure. The hind legs, strong from all that bouncing, can kick hard enough to **disembowel** a dog. Kangaroos can grow large, up to 1.5 metres for a big **Red Kangaroo**, though you're more likely to encounter the smaller Eastern or Western Greys.

Brought-over Buffalo

Water buffalo were introduced in 1825 and now cover much of the Top End, where they have a destructive effect on wetlands. Big bulls can weigh up to 1000 kilograms, and carry a hefty set of horns. But buffalo normally avoid people and are only likely to charge if injured or provoked. Buffalo are farmed for their meat, milk, cheese and hides.

Swiping Swans and Grumpy Geese

It's been said many a time that 'a swan can break a man's arm'. It's true, they can. And a woman's, and yours too if you harass them when they are raising a batch of cygnets. Their flapping wings are easily strong enough to injure you if they make direct contact. Geese, too, are liable to charge up hissing and flapping if threatened.

Black Swans *are native to Australia.*

Introduced **domestic geese** *are the ones you're most likely to meet, as they often live on farms or around lakes in city parks.*

The Other Coat-of-arms Kicker

The **Emu** is our biggest bird, and it has long legs and big feet with sharp talons. Since it can't fly, the Emu will usually run from danger. But a cornered or injured Emu, or one protecting its young, can deliver a powerful kick.

Kickers and Bruisers

Even if they don't have venom or fangs, most animals can and will do something to defend themselves if they feel threatened. Sometimes a scared or threatened animal will react in a way that causes breaks and bruises. Animals that you wouldn't usually think of as a threat (and normally they're not) can peck and kick and gouge and flap to protect themselves.

The Bloodsuckers

Many people feel a little ill at the thought of something sucking their blood. Make that something a big fat leech or a blood-swollen tick and the queasiness quota goes up. But it's not the blood coming out that should bother you—it's what might be going in. The main concern with blood-sucking **parasites** is the diseases they can spread within and between **species**—diseases that have caused more human deaths than all the world's large predators and venomous stabbers and stingers combined.

On the March

March Flies are big, slow and clumsy. This makes them easy to brush away if they land on you. The problem is you might not notice it until you feel its sting. More likely to bother you in the warmer months, March Flies bumble around from the tropics to the alps, searching for blood.

Pest or Threat?

There are over 300 **species** of **mosquito** in Australia but only about five of these are known to spread disease. Over many years malaria has killed millions of people around the world. Malaria was eradicated in Australia more than 20 years ago, but mosquito-borne diseases such as Ross River fever and dengue fever are still genuine threats to humans in our tropical north. Mosquitos usually live off plant juices but the females look for blood to feed on when they are getting ready to breed.

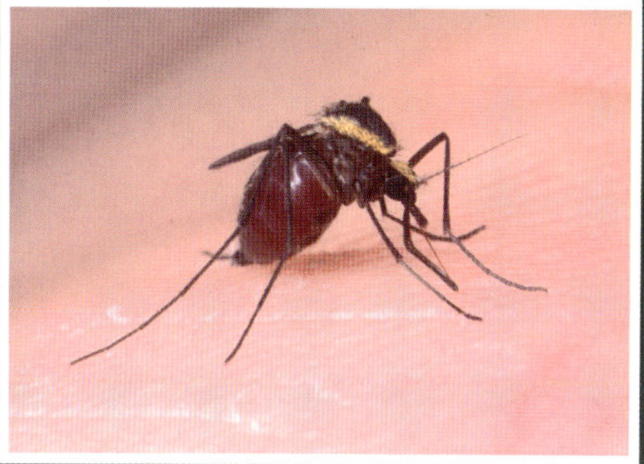

This greedy ***bush mozzie*** *is full of blood and still drinking.*

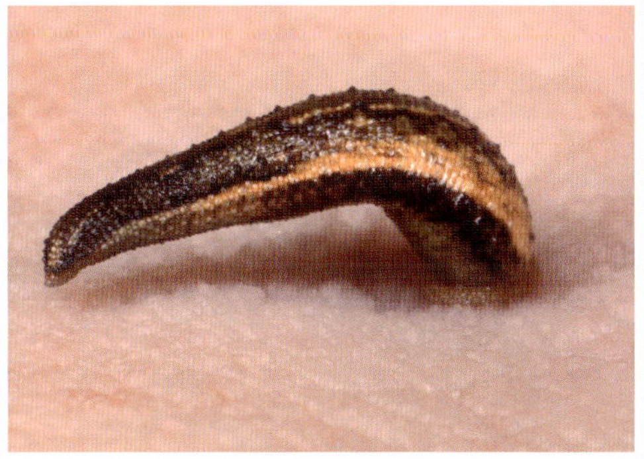

Balloons of Blood

Leeches can latch on across much of this country, but especially around damp, swampy, thickly forested areas. Their sensors pick up heat and cold, light, smell and vibrations and guide them to a suitable **host**. The leech will feed on blood until it has swollen up to five times its usual size. After about 20 minutes it will drop off to spend the next few months digesting its liquid lunch.

Leaks from a Leech

Don't ever pull a **leech** straight off you—that can tear the skin. Instead, carefully apply heat from a lighter or sprinkle on salt or vinegar to convince the leech to let go. Because the leech's saliva contains an **anticoagulant** to keep your blood flowing, the wound can continue to bleed for a few hours after the leech has been removed. The Australian land leech has two jaws, each equipped with sharp little teeth that leave a characteristic Y-shaped bite.

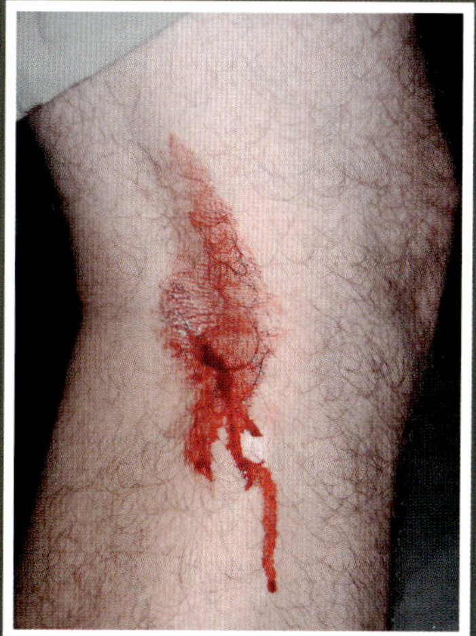

This is the dangerous ***Paralysis Tick****. It can kill your dog.*

Sticking Ticks

The east coast of Australia gets the tick for being the most likely place to find small **bush ticks**, or have them find you. Common in scrubby, shrubby country, ticks can go unnoticed, increasing the risk of them causing sickness. Removing a tick can be tricky—you'll need tweezers and a steady hand to make sure you don't leave the tick's head embedded in your flesh.

Fleas with Fangs

These little bloodsucking **parasites** once led to the deaths of over 200 million people. That was back in the fourteenth century when flea bites helped spread a plague across Europe and Asia that became known as the Black Death. These days, fleas are more of a biting, itchy hassle than a hazard. Though they can survive months without eating, both males and females will look to a variety of **hosts** from which to extract a free feed of blood.

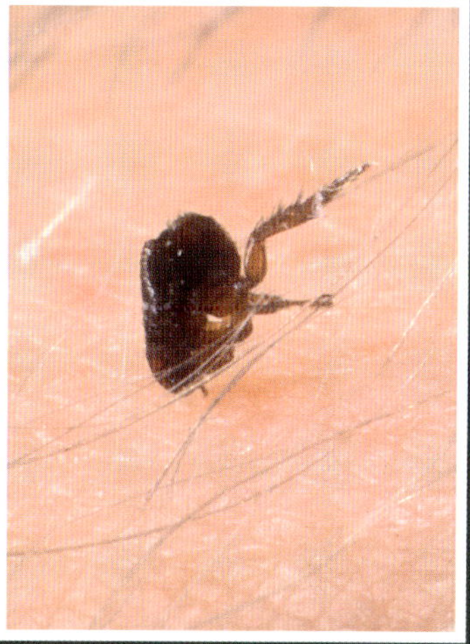

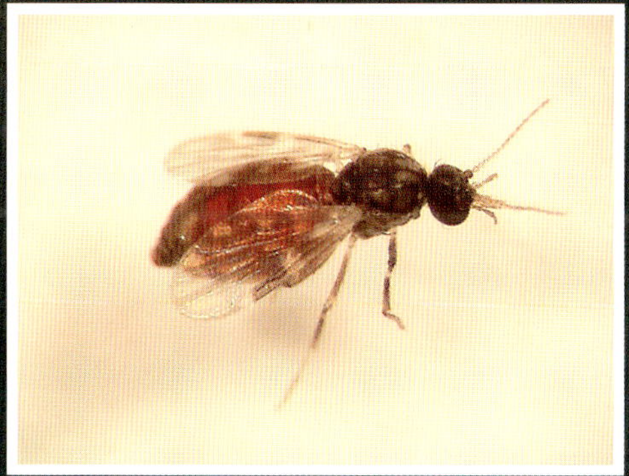

Suckers from the Sand

Just before nightfall, usually around swampy and mangrove coastal areas, small **sandflies** emerge in the thousands. These tiny flies, also known as biting midges or no-see-ums, can be an irritating addition to a summer evening, though locals often build up an immunity to the itch.

Female

Fifteen Minutes of Pain

The bite of the male Sydney **Funnel-web** can kill in a quarter of an hour. Though smaller than the female, the male's **venom** contains more of the harmful active ingredient. Males are also more mobile, often out and about on warm summer evenings searching for a mate.

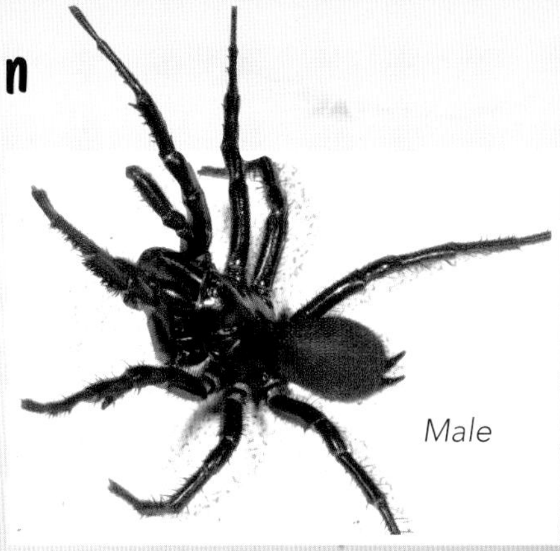

Male

Although funnel-webs are known to rush out from their burrow with forelegs raised and fangs oozing venom, they won't run up your arm and bite you. They will only bite if pressure is applied to their body, just as it would be if a predator got hold of them. We humans get bitten when a funnel-web ends up on us and we frantically, and understandably, try to brush it off. As awful and difficult as it sounds, if you just let it make its own way off, you are less likely to be bitten.

Window Weavers

The messy web of the **Black House Spider** can often be found in the corners of windows, leading to its other common name, the Black Window Spider. Bites are rare but the short-lived symptoms are striking: severe pain, giddiness, nausea and sweating. But these spiders also catch a lot of household insect pests, so the benefits of having them around the home might outweigh the minor risk of being bitten.

Wandering White-taileds

Unfortunately for them, and maybe for us, Black House Spiders are the preferred prey of **White-tailed Spiders**. This can lead to a 'home invasion' of White-taileds roaming around hunting Black House Spiders. This is when we are most likely to encounter them. Easily identified by the white spot on the tip of their **abdomens**, the bite of the White-tailed Spider causes headaches and nausea and there is evidence that it also contributes to **necrosis**.

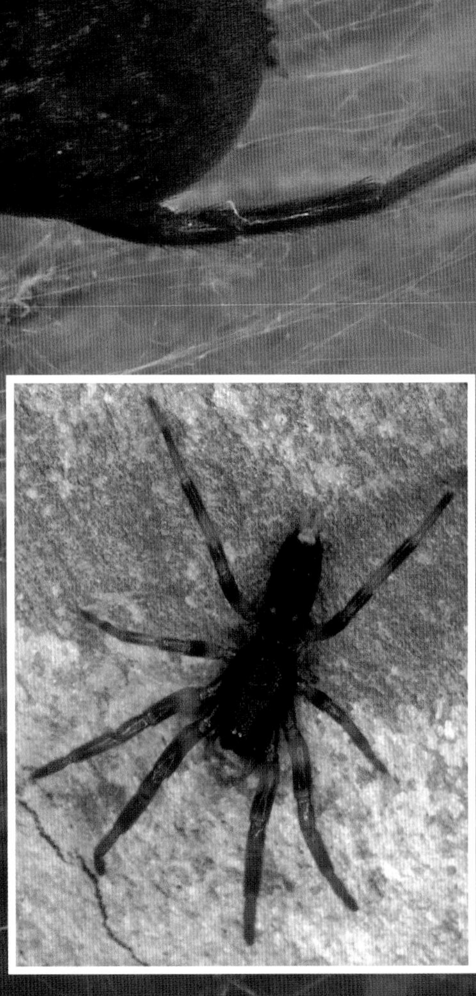

Fanged Hunters

Wandering into a spider web is a horrible experience. The silk sticks to your hands, your hair and your face. The spider, or worse, spiders, could be anywhere on you. But it's not the web-weavers you really need to worry about. Although nearly all spiders are venomous, most aboveground web-building spiders are harmless to humans. However, the bite of some of the more ancient ground-dwelling, burrowing spiders can be a real bother. They've been crawling across the planet for millions of years and have had plenty of time to **evolve** well-tested **toxins** to help keep them fed, alive and thriving. But of the 2000-plus spider **species** in Australia, only a few are dangerous to humans and even they tend to ignore us as long as we return the favour.

Red-back Relative

Although it is related to the Red-back, the **Brown House Spider's** bite usually causes nothing beyond headaches and nausea. But a few cases have turned more serious and in these situations Red-back antivenom appears to have eased the symptoms. You'll often find Brown House Spiders in your home or garden, lurking in dark secluded places.

Multicoloured Mouse

Most mouse spiders are basic black, brown or grey. The boldly coloured male **Red-headed Mouse Spider** is an exception, and it is also bold enough to bite if handled or cornered. These funnel-web relatives are not as aggressive and so are considered less dangerous. There is still a lot we need to learn about mouse spiders, but the fact that their **venom** kills baby mice quicker than that of the funnel-web makes them worth keeping away from.

Scarlet Spider

The glossy and vibrant **Red-back Spider** is, along with the funnel-web, Australia's best known and most dangerous spider. But unlike funnel-webs, it's the female that can give you a fatal bite. Male Red-backs are small and their fangs aren't big enough to pierce your skin. But the nearly 1.5-centimetre long female (pictured) can, and will, if disturbed. Web-weaving Red-backs are more 'modern' than most dangerous Australian spiders and often spin their webs in rubbish heaps and woodpiles.

Squish, Squirt, Spit and Splatter

Goo that squirts out of an insect's **abdomen** or oozes off a toad's warty skin is probably not something you want to get on yourself. It might sting, it might stink and it could be toxic. Some creatures can squirt or **secrete** chemical-loaded substances that can drive off or even kill potential predators. If you happen to get these oozes on yourself they are more likely to irritate than injure. But since all these substances are designed to cause an adverse reaction in the creature's 'enemies', it's best to avoid getting any of them on you.

Gut-spilling Cucumbers

Some **sea cucumbers** can expel their intestines, as well as toxic white sticky threads, when they're threatened or handled. These threads can irritate your eyes and skin. People also eat these slug-like animals, but unfortunately some **species** are poisonous and can cause death. Also known as beche-de-mer or trepang, over-harvesting caused the collapse of the sea cucumber industry in northern Australian.

Toxic Toads

The **Cane Toad** is a real killer. The poison glands that cover the toad's body kill many creatures that try to eat it, and those that survive rarely come back for a second try. The toad's **toxins** are only released when the animal is squeezed, which is one good reason for not picking them up. The toxin can be dangerous if it gets into your eyes or mouth so don't goad the toad.

Bright, Shiny Stinkers

Just as the name suggests, **stink bugs** (right) smell. But not all the time: the smell from these large, often brightly coloured bugs is only used to drive predators away. If you pick one up or harass it with a stick, it's likely to think you want to eat it and will stop you by releasing a foul-smelling little cloud.

Larvae with Liquid

Young **sawflies** (above) can really irritate you. The adults of these relatives of ants, wasps and bees don't have a sting. But in their **larvae** days, if they are disturbed they can **secrete** a liquid that irritates human skin. Often seen in large writhing clumps in trees, sawfly larvae are also called 'spitfires' but they don't actually spit—the irritant just oozes out.

Acid from an Ant

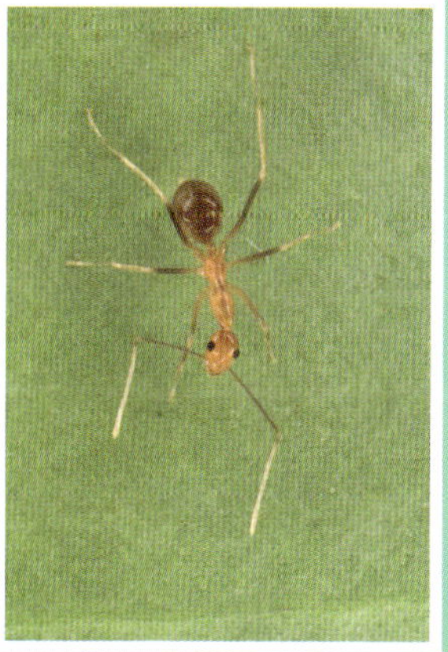

An invasion of African acid-squirting ants sounds like something from science fiction but it's happening right now. **Yellow Crazy Ants** have most likely made their way from Africa to Christmas Island, where they play havoc with the red crab populations, and then on to northern Australia, via cargo ships. But they are not the type of import we want. As wild as their name suggests, they squirt formic acid into their prey's eyes, blinding the creature. The dense colonies feed on the native plants while killing native animals or outdoing them in finding food. In Arnhem Land they've infested 25 000 square kilometres of land and their impact is being felt by local Aboriginal communities, for whom many of the same plants are an important food source.

Skin Piercers *and* Burrowers

Some animals are irritating. They can get under your skin, for real, by either burrowing in or having bits of themselves break off in you. Most of the time these burrowers and breakers are not a major health hazard: we are lucky in Australia that we don't have some of the dangerous aggressive **parasites** found in some parts of the world. But even so, some can be irritating at best and bites can be painful and slow to heal in the worst-case scenarios so avoid the burrowers if you can.

Crown-of-thorns Starfish

The **Crown-of-thorns Starfish** feeds on live corals in places like the Great Barrier Reef. Covered in sharp spines that easily break off in anything that brushes up against it, the Crown-of-thorns can cause painful, swollen and slow-healing wounds, suggesting that **venom** could also be injected. **Infestations** of this potentially destructive creature can destroy a 5-kilometre section of coral reef every month.

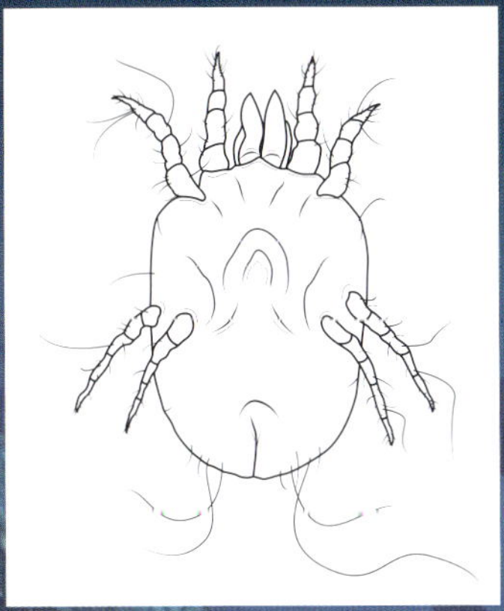

Mighty Mites

Mites are miniature, about 1–2 millimetres long, but they are almost everywhere. **Dust Mites** (illustrated) are in all homes; inhaling them or their droppings can cause problems for asthma sufferers. A bite from a mite can also be bad—in Australia's north a disease known as scrub **typhus** is transmitted by some mite **species**. Scabies Mites burrow under your skin, mate, lay eggs and die. The eggs then hatch and start the cycle again. **Infestations** of Scabies Mites can be excruciatingly itchy.

Stabbing Sea Urchins

Watch where you're walking around coastal rock pools! If you tread on the slippery spines of a sea urchin they might stick in your feet and snap off. This leaves the spines embedded in your skin, where they can cause pain and itching for days, or longer. Sometimes the spines will re-emerge a distance away from where they first went in. For the same reason picking up sea urchins is a not a good idea either. Of the 600 known **species**, 80 are believed to have **venom** that works on humans. Sea urchins come in many sizes and colours, with a variety of spine shapes and lengths.

Skin-spiking Sponges

People have used dried-out sea sponges to wash themselves for thousands of years. But you wouldn't want to do that with the **species** that are covered in sharp **spicules**. The spicules snap off in the skin and then, along with any associated **toxins**, cause dermatitis. Symptoms of this painful skin disease start at the entry site and spread from there. The pain is said to feel like 'glass ground into the skin' and the condition can last for week after painful week.

Worm Wounds

Bristle Worms might not mean to get under your skin but they can. The first line of defence is to bite, but people often have an unwanted brush with a Bristle Worm when they accidentally come up against one around coral or in sand. The brittle bristles protecting the worm's body easily pierce and then break off in the skin, resulting in rashes and other itchy, painful sores.

Spurs, Spikes and Harpoons

Humans use harpoons to hunt and so do some other predators. A range of creatures come armed with an array of spikes and **spurs** with which to get food, drive off danger, or both. Many can also inject **venom**, adding danger to the pain. These weapons are usually only used when the creatures are handled or trapped: a good reason to live and let live when you're around these stabbers.

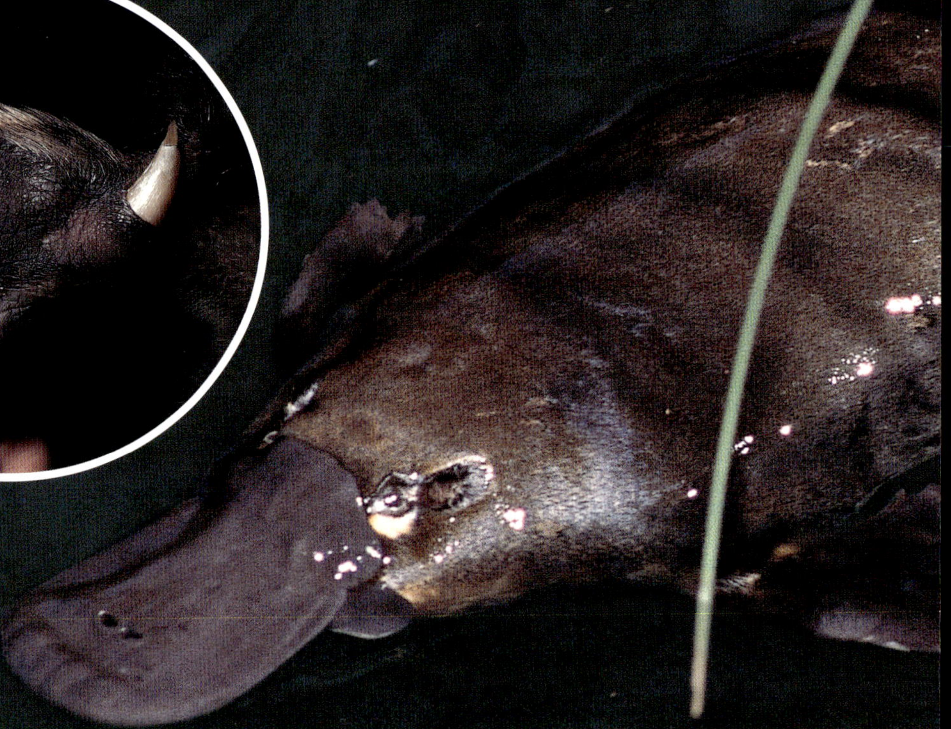

A Point to the Platypus

The male Platypus doesn't look like a well-armed creature, but it is. **Spurs** on its hind legs are mostly used as weapons in fights between rival males, but you might get stabbed if you try to catch one.The spurs are capable of injecting **venom**, which is produced in greater quantities during the breeding season. Platypuses are shy and usually only seen in the early morning or twilight hours. Stabbings are rare but are reported to produce painkiller-resistant agony.

Stab from a Stingray

A stingray stab can be very painful. If you harass or tread on a stingray in the shallows you could get spiked with the hard, pointed, serrated spine at the base of its tail. Since stingrays spend a lot of time concealed in the sand, this is how most injuries happen. The spines, often coated with **venom**, can cause deep cuts. Being brittle, they can break off in the wound, causing severe swelling.

Splitting Shrimps

If you pick up one of these bright and unusual looking shrimps you'll probably drop it pretty swiftly. Some **mantis shrimps** use their claws to crush, others to slash and impale prey. 'Split thumbs', as these 1–40-centimetre shrimps are also called, can hit you with a lightning-fast slice, causing a bit of bleeding and a lot of pain. The strike is virtually impossible to avoid, being one of the fastest animal movements measured.

Scorpion Strike

Our scorpions are not as dangerous as some overseas **species**, but you still don't want to get stung by one. Their **venom** is usually used to paralyse **insects** but two people are believed to have died from its effects. Delivered via a swift flick of the tail, the venomous sting can cause extreme pain and possible allergic reactions. Related to mites and spiders, scorpions use their eight legs to help chase down their prey.

Snails of the Sea

There's no safe way to pick up a **cone shell**. Just don't. Often found around reefs and rocky outcrops, inside these often striking-looking shells is a creature that is striking in another way. Related to land-dwelling snails, these animals are armed with a venomous barbed dart. It's attached to the cone shell's **proboscis**, a limb that can whip around in any direction to get you. The dart is used to kill prey and put off predators, including people.

Cassowary Contact

As more and more of their northern Queensland rainforest habitat is cleared for human settlement and activities, human contact with Cassowaries is more common than it used to be. As a result these big birds are losing their natural wariness and getting bolder and, therefore, more dangerous—they can deliver a powerful kick in defence of their chicks. Our steady advance into the Cassowary's territory also makes them more vulnerable to traffic.

Dead Dazzlers

The common names for some **species** of **cone shell** give an idea of their beauty—the Cloth of Gold, Pearled Cone and Tulip Cone are all sought after by collectors. But the demands of the collector market have led to fewer of many of the more striking species of cone shells. Never take shells containing live animals from the beach.

Rotten Rivers

Fortescues and frogs, kangaroos and crocodiles are all affected by pollution of our waterways. Changes to a habitat can have a negative impact on all the life that is bound up in that **food web**. In a continent as dry as ours, taking care of our waterways should be a priority, not just for us but for every-thing that depends on them to survive.

This ***Ocean Sunfish*** *is caught in a shark net.*

Net of Death

The netting of popular beaches on the Australian coast does reduce the risk of shark attacks. Sharks, including some big individuals from known suspect **species**, are regularly caught in the nets. But so are other creatures. Small or harmless sharks, turtles, dolphins and even young whales can be caught and die from a long, slow suffocation. Netting has long been accepted as part of urban coastal life but some people are beginning to question whether the benefits are outweighed by the unavoidable and unnecessary killing of large marine creatures.

Endangered Dangers

We've looked at a lot of animals that can occasionally be dangerous to us. But what about when things are the other way around, when we are the dangerous **species**? We have killed a lot more snakes, spiders, sharks, crocodiles, cone shells and corals than they have killed us. Sometimes we kill individual animals so they won't have a chance to get us first. At other times our actions can upset the balance of life for a whole species. In an effort to protect ourselves or tame 'wild' Australia we can risk endangering the very 'dangers' that add an oddly enjoyable edge to a walk through our bush or a swim in our seas.

Killer from the Cane

The **Cane Toad** does the killing but we are the ones to blame. Cane Toads were introduced over 100 years ago to eat beetles that were consuming our sugarcane crops. But the plan backfired. The toads didn't eat the beetles because they couldn't climb the cane to get them, but they did start eating just about everything else they could catch and swallow, whilst poisoning anything that tried to eat them. And they still do. As they continue their spread across the continent this tide of toxic toads is reducing the northern population of Red-bellied Black Snakes and other native creatures to worryingly low levels.

Grey Nurse, Grey Ghosts?

The widespread hunting of **Grey Nurse Sharks** in the days when they were considered to be killers has led to a serious decline in their populations. On the west coast it is classed as 'extremely vulnerable' while on the east coast the situation is even grimmer. Only 300–500 sharks are thought to exist and the **species** is listed as 'critically endangered'. Despite government protection, many marine biologists fear these graceful sharks are swimming towards extinction.

Activities

1. How many species of shark are there in Australian waters? (p. 4–5)

2. Are snakes poisonous? (p. 6–7)

3. What are wasps and bees attracted to? (p. 8–9)

4. What are nematocysts? (p. 10–11)

5. How do some fish protect themselves? (p. 12–13)

6. How do electric rays use electricity? (p. 14–15)

7. How many ant species are there? Can you name a few? (p. 16–17)

8. What birds are pictured on page 18? Have you seen them in the wild? Where? (p. 18–19)

9. Name three ways that sharks find their prey. (p. 20–21)

10. Are Moray Eels friendly? (p. 22–23)

11. What are the main differences between Saltwater and Freshwater crocodiles? (p. 24–25)

12. How many snakes might be dangerous? (p. 26–27)

13. Where are brown snakes found? (p. 28–29)

14. How do kangaroos and Emus defend themselves? (p. 30–31)

15. What is the most dangerous thing about bloodsuckers? (p. 32–33)

16. When do funnel-web spiders bite? (p. 34–35)

17. How did Yellow Crazy Ants come to Australia? (p. 36–37)

18. What happens if you tread on the spikes of sea urchins or sea sponges? (p. 38–39)

19. Are Platypuses dangerous? How? (p. 40–41)

20. Why are Cane Toads a problem? (p. 42–43)

21. Look at the Glossary on page 46. Choose a few words and find them in the book. What creatures do they refer to?

22. Go to page 47, titled Want to Know More? Choose a creature in the book and find out more about it on one of the websites.

Glossary (what words mean)

abdomen	the rear body part of an insect or spider
antibodies	substances in the blood which counteract the harmful effects of toxins or diseases
anticoagulant	a substance that prevents or slows the clotting ability of blood
aquatic	something that lives or grows in water
bacteria	tiny organisms, some of which can cause disease
billabong	a waterhole formed from a side branch of a river or creek
brackish	slightly salty water
camouflage	shapes, patterns and colours that enable creatures to blend into their background.
cnidarians	these creatures include sea anemones, jellyfish and corals
colony	a group of separate animals or plants that link up to co-exist
communal	living together in a group
crustaceans	these creatures include crabs, lobsters and prawns
disembowel	to remove the internal organs of the main body trunk
domesticated	animals that have been tamed and bred by humans
dry bite	a snake bite from a venomous snake where no venom is injected
estuarine	areas where rivers meet the sea and are subject to tides, or an inlet of the sea
evolve	to slowly change over time
family	one of the largest groupings of animals. For example, humans, gorillas, chimpanzees and orangutans are all part of the Hominid family.
food web	creatures that are interrelated by their feeding habits.
formic acid	a colourless, irritating liquid produced by some insects
genus	a subdivision of a family; a group of closely related animals (species)
host	the plant or animal on which a parasite lives
infestations	large groupings or numbers of creatures
insects	the millions of creatures with hard external protective coverings, three distinct body parts (head, thorax, abdomen), and usually with three pairs of legs and two pairs of wings
iridescent	displaying bright rainbow-like colours
larvae	young insects once they have hatched from eggs
mandibles	the main chewing and biting part of an insect's mouth
necrosis	the destruction of living tissues and organs by a toxin
nematocysts	the stinging cells of jellyfish and their relatives
nocturnal	creatures that are mostly active at night
organism	any form of animal or plant life
parasite	an animal or plant that lives on or in another living organism
proboscis	a long, flexible feeding organ
rays	type of fish, related to sharks, with flattened bodies
secrete	to release substances from the skin or other parts of the body
species	a single type of animal or plant, for example Red Kangaroo, Olive Sea Snake. Closely related species make up a genus.
spicules	the hard external skeletal part of certain animal species, often sharp and spiky
spur	a hard, sharp growth on the wings or legs of some creatures, usually used for protection
toxicity	the degree to which a creature's venom is dangerous
toxin	a substance that can be harmful to human health
typhus	an infectious disease caused by micro-organisms (only visible under a microscope) and spread by lice, mites and fleas
venom	toxin-containing fluid produced by a venomous creature

Want to Know More?

The internet isn't called the 'World Wide Web' for nothing. These days, we can access sites and information from down the road or across the globe. And there are many sites related to animals. This page lists some sites where you can go to find out more about Australia's animals, both the dangerous ones and the less alarming species.

Oodles of Zoos

Zoos were once all about putting animals on display for people to look at. But not any more. Most zoos now take much more notice of what the animal inhabitants need to keep them healthy, and happy. Though many would argue that the only place for wild animals is in the wild, modern zoos do play a major role in breeding endangered animals as well as educating the public.

http://www.zoo.org.au/
http://www.adelaidezoo.com.au/
http://www.currumbin-sanctuary.org.au/
http://www.perthzoo.wa.gov.au/index.html
http://www.zoo.nsw.gov.au/
http://www.reptilepark.com.au/
http://wmi.com.au/crocpark/
http://www.seaworld.com.au
http://www.sydneyaquarium.com.au/
http://www.aqwa.com.au/main.asp

Sites for Saving

There are many organisations and individuals who work hard to help save our planet's endangered wildlife. Some take a global outlook; others concentrate on specific species or regions. But all of them, large and small, play a crucial role in helping to preserve the Earth's wild creatures.

http://www.worldwildlife.org
http://www.wilderness.org.au/
http://www.greenpeace.org.au/
http://www.wwf.org/
http://www.hsi.org.au/

Websites with Bite

There are countless websites devoted to animals. Just do a bit of searching and you'll soon see. Listed below are a few sites where you can find out interesting facts, see some fantastic photos and get involved with interactive activities.

http://www.australianfauna.com/
http://pbskids.org/eekoworld/index_flash.html
http://www.barrierreefaustralia.com/
http://www.abc.net.au/schoolstv/animals/default.htm
http://www.kidcyber.com.au/topics/animals.htm
http://home.iprimus.com.au/readman/
http://www.kidzone.ws/

Index